To Katherine and Lawrence
Many Happy Return[illegible] love from
on [illegible] Claire.

To Carly and Nicholas with love.

British Library Cataloguing in Publication Data

Poems, prayers and graces.
    1. Children — Religious life — Juvenile literature
    I. Jennings, Linda M.   II. Gregory, Sally
248.8'2   BV4571.2

    ISBN   0-340-34873-9

This compilation © 1984 Hodder and Stoughton
Illustrations copyright © 1984 Sally Gregory

First published 1984

Published by Hodder and Stoughton Children's Books,
a division of Hodder and Stoughton Ltd, Mill Road,
Dunton Green, Sevenoaks, Kent TN13 2YJ

Printed in Hong Kong by Colorcraft Ltd

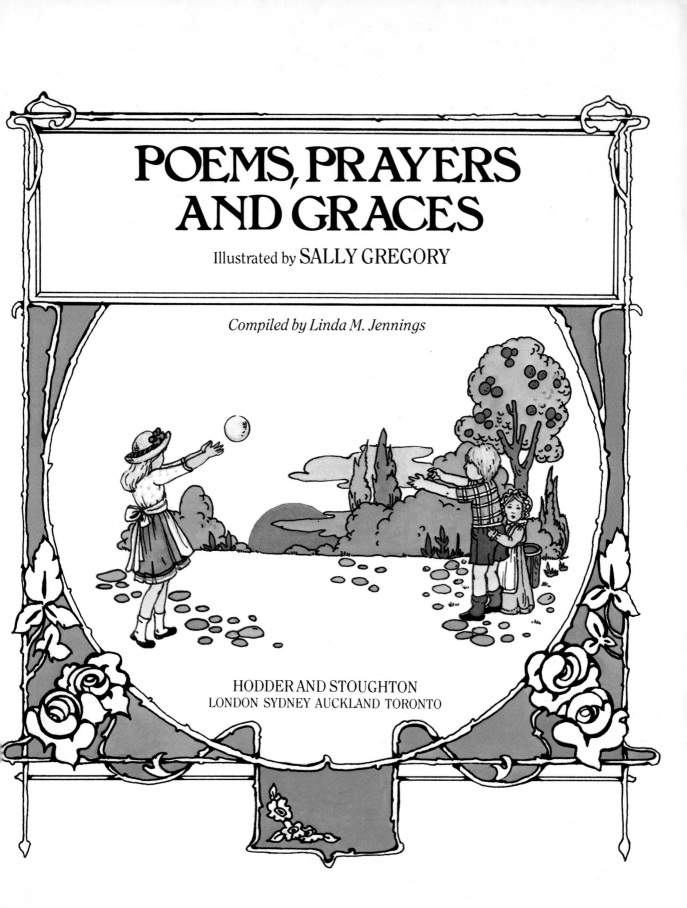

POEMS, PRAYERS AND GRACES

Illustrated by SALLY GREGORY

Compiled by Linda M. Jennings

HODDER AND STOUGHTON
LONDON SYDNEY AUCKLAND TORONTO

Matthew, Mark, Luke and John,
Bless the bed that I lie on.
Four corners to my bed,
Four angels round my head,
One to watch, and one to pray,
And two to bear my soul away.

Traditional

As the daylight follows night,
As the stars and moon give light,
So, dear Lord, with all your might,
Care for me.

As the Springtime brings the flowers,
As the minutes turn to hours,
So, dear Lord, with all your powers,
Care for me.

As with Peace the swift-winged Dove,
Looks upon me from above,
So, dear Father, with thy love,
Care for me.

Olwen T. Godwin

Thank you for the world so sweet,
Thank you for the things we eat,
Thank you for the birds that sing,
Thank you, God, for everything.

E. Rutter Leatham

All good gifts around us
Are sent from Heaven above —
Then thank the Lord, O thank the Lord,
For all his love.

Matthias Claudius
1740 — 1815

Some ha'e meat, and canna eat,
And some wad eat that want it;
But we ha'e meat, and we can eat,
And sae the Lord be thankit.

Robert Burns
1759 — 1796

God of all our cities,
Each alley, street and square,
Pray look down on every house,
And bless the people there.

Joan Gale Thomas

Let dogs delight to bark and bite,
For God hath made them so;
Let bears and lions growl and fight,
For 'tis their nature, too.

But, children, you should never let
Such angry passions rise;
Your little hands were never made
To tear each other's eyes.

Dr Isaac Watts
1674 — 1748

The sun has gone to rest,
The bee forsakes the flowers,
The young bird slumbers in its nest,
Within the leafy bowers,
Where have I been this day,
Into what folly run,
Forgive me, Father, when I pray
Through Jesus Christ, thy Son.

From a Sampler of 1857

Dear Lord, once you were very small
And felt as little children do,
And so I know you'll understand
This tiny prayer I bring to you.

You know that sometimes I forget
To do what Mummy says I should
O could you spare an Angel, Lord,
To help me to be kind and good.

I think if one watched over me
And knew the things I did and said,
The naughty thoughts would fly away,
And all the good ones come instead.

Please let the stars look down on me —
They are your candles in the night;
And God bless Dad and Mummy, too,
And keep us safe till morning light.

Muriel Arnott

Dear God,

Thank you for all my pets; for my dog who is such a good and faithful friend; for my playful kitten who makes me laugh and is so soft and warm on my lap; and for my rabbit with his beautiful long silky ears. You, dear God, who notices the fall of a single sparrow, guard and protect all animals and birds and keep them safe from harm.

Marion Sheffield

For flowers that bloom about our feet,
Father, we thank thee.
For the song of bird and hum of bee,
Father, we thank thee.
For all things fair we hear or see,
Father in heaven, we thank thee.

For blue of stream and blue of sky,
Father, we thank thee.
For pleasant shade of branches high,
Father, we thank thee.
For fragrant air and cooling breeze,
For the beauty of the blooming trees,
Father in heaven, we thank thee.

For this new morning with its light,
Father, we thank thee.
For the rest and shelter of the night,
Father, we thank thee.
For health and food, for love and friends,
For everything thy goodness sends,
Father in heaven, we thank thee.

Ralph Waldo Emerson
1803 — 1882

To God who gives our daily bread
A thankful song we raise,
And pray that he who sends us food
May fill our hearts with praise.

Thomas Tallis
1510 — 1585

O God who created and loves all creatures
I think of the animals that must work so hard,
the oxen that have to pull heavy burdens,
and the donkeys that carry big loads.

Care for the hungry donkeys
and make people kind to animals.

Child's prayer from India

Dear Father, hear and bless
Thy beasts and singing birds,
And guard with tenderness
Small things that have no words.

From Hymns and Prayers for Children

Jesus, tender Shepherd, hear me,
Bless thy little lamb tonight;
Through the darkness be thou near me,
Watch my sleep till morning light.

All this day thy hand has led me,
And I thank thee for thy care;
Thou hast clothed me, warmed and fed me,
Listen to my evening prayer.

Let my sins be all forgiven,
Bless the friends I love so well;
Take me, when I die, to heaven,
Happy there with thee to dwell.

Mary L. Duncan
1814 — 1840

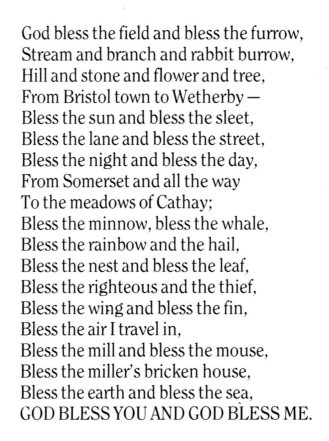

God bless the field and bless the furrow,
Stream and branch and rabbit burrow,
Hill and stone and flower and tree,
From Bristol town to Wetherby —
Bless the sun and bless the sleet,
Bless the lane and bless the street,
Bless the night and bless the day,
From Somerset and all the way
To the meadows of Cathay;
Bless the minnow, bless the whale,
Bless the rainbow and the hail,
Bless the nest and bless the leaf,
Bless the righteous and the thief,
Bless the wing and bless the fin,
Bless the air I travel in,
Bless the mill and bless the mouse,
Bless the miller's bricken house,
Bless the earth and bless the sea,
GOD BLESS YOU AND GOD BLESS ME.

Traditional

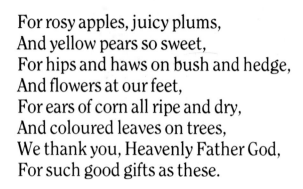

For rosy apples, juicy plums,
And yellow pears so sweet,
For hips and haws on bush and hedge,
And flowers at our feet,
For ears of corn all ripe and dry,
And coloured leaves on trees,
We thank you, Heavenly Father God,
For such good gifts as these.

From a Teacher in Hull

Make me, dear Lord, polite and kind
To everyone, I pray;
And may I ask you how you find
Yourself, dear Lord, today.

John Bannister Tabb

Be near me, Lord Jesus; I ask thee to stay
Close by me for ever, and love me, I pray;
Bless all the dear children in thy tender care,
And fit us for Heaven to live with thee there.

J. T. McFarland

Hush! my dear, lie still and slumber,
Holy angels guard thy bed!
Heavenly blessings without number
Gently falling on thy head.

Sleep, my babe; thy food and raiment,
House and home, thy friends provide;
All without thy care or payment,
All thy wants are well supplied.

May'st thou live to know and fear Him,
Trust and love Him all thy days;
Then go dwell for ever near Him
See His face, and sing His praise!

Dr Isaac Watts
1674 — 1748

God who created me
Nimble and light of limb,
In three elements free,
To run, to ride, to swim;
Not when the sense is dim,
But now from the heart of joy,
I would remember Him;
Take the thanks of a boy.

Henry Charles Beeching
1859 — 1919

Two little eyes to look to God;
Two little ears to hear his word;
Two little feet to walk in his ways;
Two little lips to sing his praise;
Two little hands to do his will,
And one little heart to love him still.

From S.U. Songs and Choruses

Jesus bids us shine
With a pure clear light,
Like a little candle
Burning in the night.
In this world of darkness;
So let us shine,
You in your small corner,
And I in mine.

Susan Warner
1819 — 1895

Where did you come from, baby dear?
Out of the everywhere into here.

Where did you get those eyes so blue?
Out of the sky as I came through.

What makes the light in them sparkle and spin?
Some of the starry spikes left in.

Where did you get that little tear?
I found it waiting when I got here.

What makes your forehead so smooth and high?
A soft hand stroked it as I went by.

What makes your cheek like a warm white rose?
I saw something better than anyone knows.

Whence that three-cornered smile of bliss?
Three angels gave me at once a kiss.

Where did you get this pearly ear?
God spoke, and it came out to hear.

Where did you get those arms and hands?
Love made itself into bonds and bands.

Feet, whence did you come, you darling things?
From the same box as the cherubs' wings.

How did they all just come to be you?
God thought about me, and so I grew.

But how did you come to us, you dear?
God thought about you, and so I am here.

George Macdonald
1824 – 1905

God be in my head,
And in my understanding;

God be in my eyes,
And in my looking:

God be in my mouth,
And in my speaking;

God be in my heart,
And in my thinking;

God be at my end,
And at my departing.

From the Sarum Missal

Oh, I've had a lovely Birthday,
Thank you for each little friend;
Though I know we all enjoyed it
Birthday parties have to end.

And I thank you for my presents,
And for everyone so dear;
Please God, bless and make them happy
Till my Birthday comes next year.

Hilda I. Rostron

From ghoulies and ghosties and long-leggety beasties
And things that go bump in the night,
Good Lord, deliver us!

Traditional

Good night! Good night!
Far flies the light;
But still God's love
Shall flame above,
Making all bright.
Good night! Good night!

Victor Hugo
1802 — 1885

Acknowledgements

The Editor and Publishers are grateful to the following for the use of copyright material:

WI Books Ltd and Ms Olwen T. Godwin for 'As the Daylight Follows Night' from *A Book of Childhood Prayers and Verses,* compiled by Carolyn Martin and published by Hodder and Stoughton Ltd: New Century Publishers Inc. for 'A Child's Prayer from India' from *Children's Prayers from Other Lands* by Gladys Spicer Fraser © 1954: Miss Hilda I. Rostron for 'Oh I've had a Lovely Birthday': the Scripture Union for 'Two Little Eyes' from *Scripture Union Songs and Choruses:* Marion Sheffield for 'Thank You for all my Pets': A.R. Mowbray and Co. Ltd and Joan Gale Thomas for 'God of All our Cities' from *God of All Things:* WI Books Ltd and the author for 'For Rosy Apples, Juicy Plums' from *A Book of Childhood Prayers and Verses* compiled by Carolyn Martin and published by Hodder and Stoughton Ltd. We are also grateful to Mrs Gertie Bragg for the use of the words from a sampler in her possession, 'The Sun has Gone to Rest'.